Lyrics of a Broken Heart

A Father's Journey Toward Wholeness

James Mueller

Jim Mueller aptly describes his pieces as "lyrics of a broken heart." The vulnerability on these pages about the process of grieving will forge a pathway from heart to heart and create a shared connection of understanding and deep humanity. This beautiful book will let you know that no matter how deep your grief, you are not alone in this world. It's a beautiful and necessary book that ultimately offers healing and hope.

> **Donna Gephart, award-winning author of *Lily & Dunkin*, *In Your Shoes*, and *The Paris Project***

Jim's heartfelt words will undoubtedly be the cornerstone for so many people who are experiencing the pain and difficulty of an ill loved one. There is no how-to guide on how to deal with grief, but I know this book will lay the framework for others to trust the process and have faith.

> **Ashley Brown, Founder and CEO, Selfless Love Foundation**

Through his poignant and soulful poetry and prose, Jim has shared the essence of who Luke is and was in the world and his own journey. May this precious book bring comfort and inspiration to all who are dealing with loss and the joys and challenges of having a special needs child.

> **Richard Damien, author of *A Monk in the World***

Lyrics of a Broken Heart is nothing less than a lamentation, coming from the depths of a broken spirit, over a father's loss of his son. It's not often that males allow others, especially strangers, to witness their raw emotions, but Mueller does so in this short volume. The grief, pain, and darkness are palpable as is his transition to a better place and what it took to get there. Mueller's journey, filled with struggle, is also filled with insight and hope and will serve as a support and inspiration to others who find themselves in similar situations. Equally important is what we learn about Luke, a child with severe limitations and totally dependent on others, and the place he held in the family's and others' lives. Even with all his infirmities, he was a gift to all who were graced by his presence—a poignant lesson in a society that so often insists on perfection.

> **Ron Hamel, PhD, Theologian/Ethicist**

This book is amazing—so devastating in the beginning and then so filled with light and hope at the end. Everyone who has suffered a loss should read it!

Lynn Meister, MD, Medical Director, Pediatric Palliative Care Team, Pediatric Hematologist/Oncologist, Joe DiMaggio Children's Hospital

This book addresses often-overlooked aspects of parenting: a father's perspective and love for his child. Jim Mueller's insights and reflections are worth their weight in gold. This short book is packed with words of wisdom for all dads, and especially those who may have a child with special needs.

David Hirsch, President, 21st Century Dads Foundation and host of the Special Fathers Network Dad to Dad Podcast

Jim Mueller's heart-wrenching account of the loss of his son is a stunning and soulful expression of the ultimate interpersonal loss that can be experienced by human beings. It reflects not only the sad journey that was taken by Jim, Margot, and Lili, and Jessica, but is also a tribute to Luke's bright spirit, humor, and ability to maintain an amazing family cohesiveness. Jim, as a loving father and devoted friend to Luke, has captured the essence of human devotion, love, hope, and emotional pain that only a parent can experience. Lyrics of a Broken Heart *is mandatory reading for any parent who has experienced the loss of a child.*

Robert Shumaker, PhD, Clinical Psychologist

Jim has honored Luke by the way he created this book, going deep inside to relive his own memories of joy, companionship, and love, and to confront and express without mediation the pain of the loss that adjoins the extinguishing of Luke's light. This book, like Luke's life, brings us smack up against the most fundamental questions of what we each are capable of experiencing, feeling, and enduring as we do our best to live fully in the world.

Jerry de Jaager, Luke's friend and author of *The Million Dollar Parrot: 35 Brief Stories for Big Breakthroughs*

Lyrics of a Broken Heart is a brave and courageous accomplishment. Jim Mueller allows the reader to journey along the path of extreme emotional darkness, despair, and pain to a place of light, hope, and healing. The loss of a child by a parent is arguably the toughest emotional and physical stress that can be experienced. This series of writings exposes the conscious and unconscious struggles that the psyche must overcome to resolve significant conflict or loss.

Eric S. Rutstein, MD, Psychiatrist, Founder of the Center for the Integration of Psychotherapy and Psychopharmacology in Boca Raton, Florida

Lyrics of a Broken Heart: A Father's Journey Toward Wholeness—The title says it all. Jim takes us on a journey through grief. His book will help readers realize grief work is HARD WORK. The author not only speaks of his pain of enduring his son's decline but tells how this tragic family event affects his wife and their daughters. The style of writing is engaging: a poem, an observation, then a reflection on what he has learned; and his feelings are acknowledged. In a later reflection, Jim recognizes the good/positive aspects of his son's life that can be identified. He and his family realize that the full-time care of their son is over and they need to find a new purpose in life.

Barbara Kuntz, RN, CNS, PhD, Thanatology, Hospice Volunteer

I have been a nurse for more than twenty years and specialized in hospice care for at least ten years. As a hospice nurse, I dealt with many unique families, however when I met the Mueller's family, Luke immediately occupied a special space in my heart that could never be forgotten. I remember his handsome smile that lit up the room. His mother Margot, provided phenomenal care to him. The love demonstrated by both parents in the house made the process less stressful. As for his father, Jim, I noticed the bond between a father and his son. I witnessed how bright Luke's smile gleamed throughout the room the moment his dad walked in. Luke meant so much to me, especially as we shared the same birthday. I always looked forward to visiting him and his family. He will always be remembered.

Nurlande Dejean, Hospice Nurse

Dedication

Though this is a dad's story, a true hero is Luke's mom. It has always amazed me how children naturally flock to Margot. They sense something very special in her—something that children in their innocence don't filter out. Whether in a park, at the beach, in the mall, or just walking down the street—they notice her, they look, smile, and sometimes offer gooey treats that they have been enjoying. Her beautiful smile and bright eyes light up and kids know they are safe and loved.

In whatever ways Luke thrived, it was because his mother deeply cherished him and all that he was. She was his advocate and champion. I often joked that she was the founder of BAM—bold-advocate mothers—because she was never deterred, never backed down, always pressed forward with a polite determination that was admirable to watch. She was never rude, never overbearing. But she was extraordinarily well-informed about everything related to Luke's well-being—and I mean extraordinarily. Just ask any of his doctors, allied healthcare practitioners, teachers, school administrators, education specialists, or medical equipment providers with whom she interacted. She was never defeated and relentlessly pressed forward and every day she researched, read, explored, and learned.

She was undaunted.

Those who have had the fortune of being known by her are the beneficiaries of one of life's greatest gifts.

Acknowledgments

Luke's life was full of people who cared about him and for him: from the dedicated nurses and physicians at Lutheran General Hospital neonatal intensive care unit in Park Ridge, Illinois—who helped him come into our lives; to his teachers, aides, and friends at school—like Art Wagner who loved Luke and came to spend time with him in his last days with us; to Dr. Lynn Meister and her palliative care team at Joe DiMaggio Children's Hospital in Hollywood, Florida—who helped him transition out of our lives.

In the last few years of Luke's life, there was a very special care provider at Joe DiMaggio that stood out—even among all of the special people on that team. Gerard Minor PA was always available and responsive, always kind and concerned as he helped us traverse the healthcare landscape for Luke.

The team at VITAS hospice, particularly Luke's nurse Nerlande Dejean who shared his birthday, was extraordinarily supportive and fully attuned to our needs. Special people like Nerlande have infused our lives with such a deep appreciation for care givers who grasp the meaning of caring.

Richard Damien, Luke's godfather, has been there constantly for me over Luke's lifetime and after his death, providing encouragement and emotional support. His unwavering belief that this work is invaluable to others provided the impetus for me to continue, especially at those times when doubt crept in.

Jerry de Jaager, an accomplished writer, and friend for decades, patiently reviewed numerous drafts, providing invaluable feedback and insight—he has always been emotionally present and authentic.

Donna Gephart, an award-winning children's book author, encouraged me to continue writing, but most of all I want to acknowledge her kind friendship with Lili—recognizing that the sibling can feel less important during this time of loss. When Luke died, Donna not only reached out to Lili, but she reached out to her network of authors, who sent books and words of encouragement to Lili letting her know how much they cared.

There are also those people like Charlie Hall, Susan Peirce, and Terrie Temkin with whom I shared this project, who offered insights that encouraged me to continue writing when my energy flagged.

A note of appreciation goes out to the advancement team at Joe DiMaggio Children's Hospital—Kevin Janser, Felicia Bell, and Don Eachus—who helped us establish a fund at the hospital in Luke's name. It was Felicia Bell who, during one of Luke's visits to the hospital, stopped by to listen and learn, to be present with us, to understand the challenges. That one act of lovingkindness kindled an interest in a fund at the hospital, because we knew that Felicia embodied the character and values of the institution.

And finally, the professional who translated my words and intentions into the beautiful book you are reading today: Stephen Nill is not only a brilliant editor, designer, and musician, he is a kind and caring human being—qualities that have made this book significantly better.

Foreword

Edelweiss. A small, white, clean, bright flower that is happy to meet you every morning. That was Luke and that was Luke's favorite song, and one of mine. That was how he, his family, and I developed a life-long bond several years ago, when I was consulted as Luke's palliative care physician.

Luke suffered from birth from a life-limiting chronic illness. At the time we met, he was being hospitalized frequently for unexplained refractory abdominal pain. He was in need of palliative care to provide an added layer of support to him and his family.

I provided support to Luke, his mother Margot, his father Jim, and his sister Lili for several years. The goal of palliative care is to improve the quality of life of patients with life-threatening illnesses and their families by providing expert pain and symptom management, psychosocial and spiritual support, coordination of care, and goals-of-care counseling.

I often talked with Luke's family about their wishes for him. They always focused on his quality of life. They wanted him to live as well as he could for as long as he could. They knew they probably could not add years to his life, but they strove to add life to his years.

As Luke's condition progressed, and it was apparent he was suffering, Margot, Jim, and Lili realized it was time to let him go. During that summer they enrolled him in home hospice care. Patients in hospice often live longer than we think because they are so well cared for and have more of a will to live. Luke, made as comfortable as possible, enjoyed eighteen months at home with his family, until an evening in December when he quietly left us. Since his transition, Luke's memory has lived on. His parents ensured his legacy with the establishment of the Luke Andrew Mueller Pediatric Palliative Care and Integrative Medicine Fund at Joe DiMaggio Children's Hospital. This was just one path they took in their ongoing journey to understanding their grief. In my thirty years as a Pediatric Hematologist/Oncologist and ten years as a Pediatric Palliative Care physician, I have learned that everyone grieves differently. There is no right way or wrong way to grieve.

Margot dedicated herself to Luke throughout his all-too-short life. She is an extraordinary woman who, amid her sorrow, courageously accepted the difficult decisions, always ensuring that Luke received the best possible care, taking the lead on making hospice arrangements. She embodied an extraordinary ability to be present with Luke and his caregivers, even in the most emotionally difficult times.

    Jim, always the more introspective, private parent, wrote this book to facilitate his healing and to honor his son. It reveals one man's painful quest to learn how to live with his loss. While everyone grieves differently and at their own pace, with many steps forward followed by some steps back, the journey toward renewed hope exemplified in Jim's poems and revelations will be inspiring to many others on the path—and not just parents, but anyone who has lost a loved one. I think it will resonate with many and help them to see that there are many unique ways to grieve. This book is just one tool to keep in the toolbox, and I recommend it highly to families who are experiencing grief, moving toward healing, and searching for meaning.

Lynn Meister, MD
Medical Director
Pediatric Palliative Care Team
Pediatric Hematologist/Oncologist
Joe DiMaggio Children's Hospital

Luke

Our son Luke died on a December evening at the age of twenty-one, after receiving hospice care in our home for almost eighteen months. His short life was filled with challenges, but for those who knew him, he evoked love and inspiration.

On the day that we accepted hospice care for Luke, I felt I had crossed a threshold into a place of sadness. Grief overtook me, and I mourned the loss long before it happened. This new and altered world was lived in moments. I became profoundly aware of Luke's voice, desires, movement, and discomfort.

I wrote "My Son, My Light" (next page) a few months before Luke passed. It was one of two dozen pieces I wrote in the ensuing months. The loss of Luke was dissociating and unhinging. I was groping in the darkness, in sadness, with no sense of how to move forward in a life without my son. The writing was the key to my sanity. As I continued to write, I discovered I was creating a pathway through grief toward emotional wholeness.

My Son, My Light

There is a hole in my heart where my son once lived
Laughing and giggling to his favorite song

Through the hole in my heart my soul seeps out
Longing to touch the tuft of his hair
Sense the wisp of his breath
Feel him softly nestled upon my chest

The hole in my heart lets in a cold chill
I shudder and ache with its uncivilized pain
It numbs me to sleep, then gores me awake
Thrusting its dull ignorance into my soul

As his body relinquishes its grasp of him
I imagine his essence converging with light
The light he so brilliantly embodied for us
The light that has brightened our lives

I float for now, for there is no other course
Longing for solace, the awful forgetfulness of time's cruel balm
The fading of the pain with the fading of the memory
The tuft, the breath, the nestling on my chest

During his life, Luke evoked feelings of innocence, joy, and exuberance for life, even when others in his family were feeling down. He had a knack for pulling us out of our worries and into the present, where we feel most alive.

We picked Luke's name months before he was born—naïve of what was to come. We wanted his name to have significance, so we researched the root meanings of several names and finally decided on Luke Andrew. Luke, derived from the root word "lucere," or light, and Andrew, from valiance or courage.

Shortly after his birth, Luke developed a condition known as NEC, necrotizing enterocolitis, which required surgery in the first week of his life to remove portions of his bowel that was literally coming apart. Though he miraculously recovered, the traumatizing effects of the condition severely compromised his sight, speech, and mobility. He was dependent on us for every self-care need that we usually take for granted. Though we had hopes early on, he was never able to support his weight to crawl or walk. Because of his spastic quadriplegia, he was not able to feed himself or care for his bodily needs. And as he moved through his teens, he experienced episodes of seizures, which we were able to control with medication. But there was little we could do as his digestive system began to deteriorate. He also experienced significant pain and it was very difficult to identify its source.

Despite these limitations, he was present with us, able to learn, and enjoyed relating to others with a simple, often loud, but endearing, "Hi!" Few could resist a reply. As one of his physical therapists said after he passed: "Luke didn't miss a thing." His infectious laughter was an expression of his spirit. Luke's moments of joy were nearly pure joy. And this was true of all his expressions. Being with Luke was like being connected to the primal source of life itself. His laughter, anger, sadness—every emotion—had an untarnished quality of authenticity without filters.

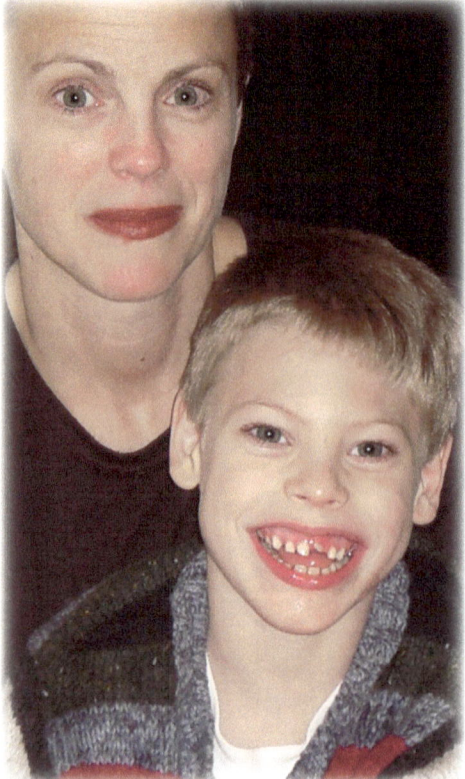

Luke's mom, Margot, was his primary caregiver for twenty-one years. She became an expert on his physical challenges and made sure he received the best medical care, was supported by appropriate technology, and was integrated into the public-school system. Throughout the seemingly countless ventures to hospitals, which usually meant myriad tests and procedures, Margot stayed at his bedside, day and night, sleeping on the couch in his hospital room, singing his favorite songs, and comforting him through all of the invasive procedures of blood draws, MRIs, EKGs, PET scans, and surgeries. Sometimes this lasted a week, sometimes longer—but she never left his side.

Through the years, we often didn't have a medical solution for Luke's challenges, or know how well we were addressing the underlying systemic pain he was suffering. But his mom was there, with little sleep, completely devoted, doing all that she could to make him comfortable. At home, she slept in his room, turning him when he needed, and again, singing or reading to him—comforting him when he couldn't sleep. I can still hear her singing Luke's favorite songs to him. The moment he made his transition, Margot was reading to him while I sat beside them. It was beautiful, but devastatingly sad.

Luke's younger sister is Lili. Though seven years his junior, from a young age she was his defender. If anyone said something unkind, she read them the riot act. She would get angry; and then sad as she struggled to understand why kids would act this way.

Even though it was hard to connect to Luke because of his limited communication ability, he still found ways to mess with his sister. To help him communicate, Margot programmed Luke's iPad with several phrases and connected it to a switch strapped to his leg. On one occasion, when the three of them were out shopping,

My Brother

The constant pinging,
Equivalent to the annoyance of a seatbelt warning
The pinging of Wheel of Fortune and Jeopardy!
And I still love you

Your tiny nose,
Your tousled hair,
And I still love you

Your scar-covered skin,
From countless surgeries and operations,
And I still love you

Your uncontrollable laugh,
Whenever you hear clapping,
The one that makes the whole room feel light
And I still love you

Your mournful cries in the dark,
The cries due to your hatred of being alone
And I still love you

Your different brain,
The one plagued with cerebral palsy
But I, and everyone who meets you, still love you

Margot asked Lili to stay with Luke while she ran into a store. She had programmed his switch to say, "I want a different song," and told Lili to just play the radio and change it if he hits his switch. When she returned Lili told her that every time she played a song, Luke hit his switch—and then he would start laughing.

For an assignment in her communication class, Lili wrote a tribute to Luke (opposite page). She was twelve at the time.

Lili would read to Luke from his favorite stories as he lay in his bed. Yet, out of all that she has given to him and done for him, she still wonders if she could have done more. And it makes her sad that she didn't finish the last book they were reading together.

Luke's older sister is ten years his senior. By the time Luke was seven, Jessica was already off to college. While she has not played a major role by being physically present in his life, his loss was no less devastating to her. As she and I reminisced, she told me stories I had forgotten, like the time on a family vacation, where she created a game with Luke that had him laughing hysterically. The game was "Dad is goofy." I wonder why I don't remember it.

Jessica also recalled one of her favorite memories as she watched Luke almost ecstatically happy as he listened to the

Moments

Sweet essence permeating my consciousness
Vibrant and delightful as his body fails
Present in the moment
Yet here, then gone
Balanced between my world and his dream

Which is the reality
Which will it be
Will he linger in my realm
Or slip away to another
It is strangely peaceful, yet pain loiters in my heart

I catch my breath
Remembering to breathe
Beckoning my consciousness back to the moment
The place where we still commune
And connect with a quiet peacefulness

It is then I can remember
His life is not mine
And the joy that he offers
Is a gift to receive
Moment by moment by moment

favorite song of his youth, "Sk8er Boi," by Avril Lavigne. Yes, that is a happy memory.

Luke was not only a son and a brother; he was a friend. While I was out most days working and building my business, he and I hung out in the evenings and weekends. Our favorite activity was sitting together watching action movies. Though we often drove to movie theaters—Sunday mornings were the best—occasionally this was difficult. Luke had sensory integration issues and loud noises caused him to become disoriented. This was aggravated by his compromised digestive system, which could cause severe pain.

As Luke aged, we made fewer trips to the theater. To compensate, we purchased a large flat screen TV and built up our action movie video library—nearly two hundred movies. I'm not sure how many movies we actually watched through to the end; oftentimes, as we watched them in the afternoon on weekends, we'd doze off with his head on my chest. Those are some of the sweetest moments in my memory.

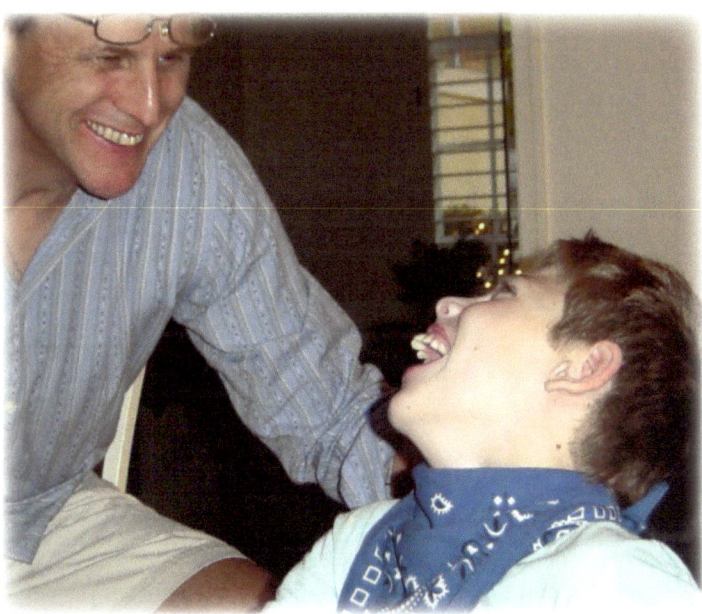

Luke was also well known at the local building supply store where he made friends with many of the kind people who worked there. He was always quick with his "Hi," which meant I had to make acquaintances with people. Margot would find this humorous—that I would actually have a conversation with someone outside of my work.

Margot has similar stories of Luke's friends at Target. Luke enjoyed—as Lili calls it—"the Target Experience," and for Luke and his mother shopping became a social event. One of Margot's fond memories is Luke's impatience when conversations with people went on too long. He'd start with just a soft "hey" reminder that he felt it was a waste of time—and the longer the conversation went on, the louder his "heys" would become.

There were times of frustration, too. Sometimes he would cry in pain, unable to tell us what was wrong. Or his issues demanded that we stop doing whatever we were engaged in, no matter how important or urgent, to take care of his needs. And yes, we lost patience, occasionally raising our voices in frustration. One or our favorite memories, ironically, is related to this. One time, out of total frustration, one of us yelled, "Geez, Luke! What is it?" Apparently, this was one of the funniest things he had ever heard, and he burst out laughing. And it became a thing for us—one of our laugh lines. If things were getting a little tense, one of us would say it, Luke would laugh, and we all would follow suit. And, sometimes I would say it just to hear him laugh.

This experience affected our family in a deeper way—some of the things we thought were so urgent, weren't. With Luke, it was a series of opportunities to let go, live in the moment, and stop worrying about what was, in essence, inconsequential.

As it became clear that Luke wasn't going to be with us much longer, I discovered a way to understand how I was feeling and to use it to process my grief. The way I found was writing, stream of consciousness from my heart. It is akin to poetry, though more accurately these pieces are the lyrics of a broken heart. I was surprised at times by what I discovered about myself. By opening my heart to express its pain I was able to avoid repressing thoughts and feelings—and by doing so, to better understand myself.

For almost eighteen months before he transitioned, Luke was experiencing neural atrophy and his body was gradually weakening. It was almost as if his presence was slowly melting away from our lives. As his condition progressed, we all vacillated on a razor's edge of hope and acceptance. We wanted each experience with him to extend for eternity—and in some ways time both ceased and accelerated. We experienced infinite moments, as if we were connecting soul to soul; then they would pass, and so did time.

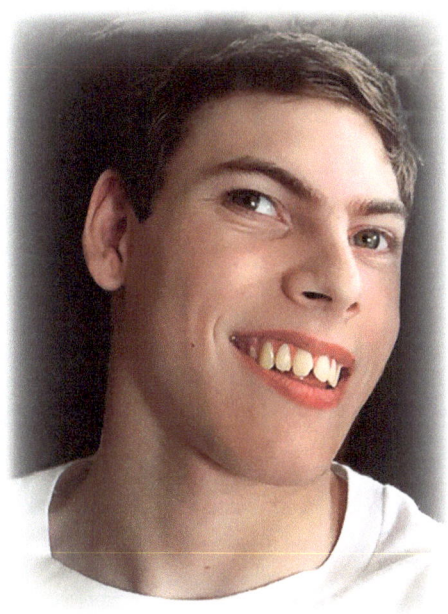

It was difficult not to worry and my mind wandered to the inevitable sadness ahead. But in the presence of Luke, I could pull myself back to the moment. And in that space, there was an ability to let go, to allow him to have his own path, to choose to live in the moments and receive the joy that resided there.

Grief: The Moment Luke Left Us

There is no bottom to the depth of my loss
No solace of kind words can assuage my pain
Infinite, lost, forever abandoned
Alone, adrift, floating in a twilight fog
Seeing feelings as they waft through my consciousness
Gut wrenching spasms of loneliness
As I watch my mortal frame from a detached distance
How odd it is to view
So sad, yet so numb
Beaten and battered by wave upon wave of lost love
Gone, alone, dark, quiet pain

On December 1st at about half past five in the afternoon, we lost Luke from this life. I've not known a more painful experience. I felt gutted, lost, and in the depth of pain—and there was no refuge. Only gut-wrenching spasms of sobbing, loneliness, and loss. My heart broke, my body trembled, and my sense of well-being shattered. For me, emotional detachment was a defense mechanism against the realization that my child was gone from my life.

No matter what I believed about life beyond death, the loss was inescapable and as real as the wall that I crumpled against in my pain and agony. There was no solace, for there was no surrogate for Luke, who was no more. I relinquished control as the waves of realization coursed through my mind and body, violent at first and then reducing to dark, quiet pain.

Amid the pain and grief, my mind turned to reflect on the devotion our family invested in Luke. There was comfort in the memory of being with him, wholly and without restraint. I know we lived well for Luke. Margot, Lili, and I had helped him through his transition by being present moment to moment, especially during his year and a half in hospice. I don't know whether Luke thought about his mortality or the implications of his condition. I do know that he wanted to be with us, as he lived longer than expected—through the pain of bed sores and compromised body functions. Near the end, I would sleep in his room in a lounge chair, just to hear him peacefully sleep—knowing these were the moments he was free of pain.

The days following Luke's death were surreal, with my emotions collapsing inward. It was very difficult to intellectually grasp the loss. Sadness engulfed me, but those sad memories remained my connection to Luke. Sometimes it felt that if I sat long enough with my sadness I would be able to reconnect to him. Or possibly discover an alternate path, a way through the loss to something new—to discover and solve the mystery that would make me feel whole again.

Ghosts

The sadness returns and beckons me
"Sit with me, contemplate my presence
"Know me and be transformed
"Know me and become real
"Know me and be"

Sadness, grieving
The weight of nothingness that once was my son
Ghosts, fleeting memory

The sad memories were only a remnant of my relationship with Luke, for they had no substance. They were fleeting echoes of what once was real. This realization was another step along the path.

This process of being present with my thoughts, watching them unfold, immersing myself fully in the emotion, was a discipline that helped me move forward in what was for me an honest process. It wasn't one of self-indulgence as I was not stuck in remorse, lost in nostalgia, or burying difficult emotions. Rather, for me it was this process of plumbing the depths of unknown grief, feeling for and finding pathways that lead outward and upward to a sense of well-being—where I hoped to emerge, though wounded, as a stronger person.

Numb

My heart no longer beats, it thumps
With the heaviness of grief
Echoing in its grey, shallow place in my chest
That is damp from tears of loss

I breathe out to keep the lonely thoughts at bay
Pushing them away with a heaving sigh
Emptying the emptiness into the atmosphere
Hoping it will disappear into the vapors

Praying the ache will relinquish its strangling grasp
That the thumping echo will calm
That the gray dampness will lighten
That I might slip into a numb nothingness of peace

Depleted

I am bled dry from sadness.
My heart cannot ache any more.

As the reality of the loss continued to seep into my consciousness, as the fog lifted, I became aware of the physicality of the loss—how it felt in my body. I realized that the contest with sadness was not a battle that could be won or even fought. For there was no enemy. But I strove to find respite, for otherwise I felt I would be pulled under and drowned. In the end, I found relief in emotional exhaustion. Being bled dry was not such a bad thing; numbness was a reprieve.

Melancholy

Melancholy has always come to me
Easier than happiness
Now that my son has died
It is my quiet refuge

    From the impositions of the kind words of others
    From the nods of understanding that are too much to bear

After three months, it became more bearable to be alone by myself. My numbness evolved to melancholy—which was a familiar experience from my childhood. It was like traveling to the hidden places where I would go as a child to be alone, to be safe.

I realized that to retreat into melancholy was part of my process of grieving—my need to live with the reality of the loss in my own way, beyond the eyes of judgment. I discovered that some wanted me to behave in a certain way—a way that was comfortable and acceptable to them. Sometimes their advice would be couched in kind words. At other times, the condolences only served to evoke a keen sense of our loss—when I would feel the thumping of my heart in a damp, grey, shallow place in my chest and the heaviness of grief that felt overwhelming in the moment.

My safety, my refuge, was to withdraw. Though I was not lost in that place, it was my way of sorting things out—to not deny my feelings, but to absorb them fully. Then carefully find openings to reach resolution, or even recognition of my new reality that allowed me to move to a more hopeful place.

When Luke passed, I had a thriving consulting practice. In the months following Luke's death, as I retreated into myself, my practice shrunk. In time I found I could compartmentalize my grief and be present with my clients. But it took time for my practice to recover.

Journey Along the Edge

There is no sure refuge from the sadness and pain
Only a delicate shell that protects my heart

As I see a photo or hear a story
Fissures and cracks form in this fragile rampart

I breathe a soft sigh, once, then again
Sending a healing vibration to strengthen my defenses

Still the sadness permeates and seeps in
Coloring my soul a grey-blue hue

Though I wished the process of grief would pass, that I would get "through it," I discovered how fragile I was, that I couldn't rush it. The emotional vulnerability did not wane quickly. It was surprising to experience how the keen, piercing pain of Luke's passing could be provoked simply by a picture or a word. It could ambush me when I least expected it—when I was least prepared. I learned that I could not defend against it, that it will seep in and evoke my sense of loss. Though I didn't admit or even see it at the time, I believe it is part of the healing process—or at least an undeniable reality. Each day as I moved forward, I could take in a bit more of reality and be okay with it.

Love, Loss, Generosity

The penalty of love is loss
Yet the feeling of loss, with its unfathomable depths
Can be transmuted through the act of generosity
The loss becomes a gift
That gift plus the grace afforded by time
Is a healing balm to all who are touched by it

For me, the intimate connection between love and loss is intense. The two are inseparable. If I open myself to love, I open myself to loss. One day, as we were getting off the elevator at Joe DiMaggio Children's Hospital, a mother with two children in tow simply said, "I wish we were getting off at the third floor." I was a bit puzzled until Margot said, "She is headed up to pediatric intensive care and oncology." Her pain, disappointment, and sorrow were all captured in a few simple words. As she disappeared behind the elevator doors, my hope was that she might find support and solace.

    A few months after Luke died, we found a way to provide support and solace to others, and along the way discovered something quite remarkable: we could transmute the nature of loss into something restorative. I wrote "Love, Loss, Generosity" for the dedication of a fund we, and many generous friends, established at Joe DiMaggio Children's Hospital. Scores of people attended, a recognition of Luke's impact on our community. The purpose of the fund was to provide support to children and their families who were facing serious illness. Through making this contribution our loss became a gift to help others; it was a powerful healing balm. And now Luke's legacy would live on to help other families as they faced similar circumstances.

The Cavern of My Lament

I've sealed the cavern of my untold grief
Yet I sleeplessly and jealously guard its entry

It is a secret place
In which I keep my memories
The comfortable clothes of a past life
The years with my friend now gone

But the taste of the memories has now turned bitter
They taste like poison on my tongue
Chilling my body and stealing my breath
Reminding me of my loss

I peel back the seal from time to time
To assure myself that I'm not callous
In imprisoning my memories safely
Away from my wounded heart

His body is now ashes
That I keep in a cabinet
The Luke I knew
Is gone from my life on earth

I believe he is happy and filled with joy
But he doesn't write and he doesn't call
The Luke that I knew is no more
He has changed, transformed, and is free

Like Narcissus I stare in the pool
Seeing only my sad reflection
I long for the day when my indulgence wanes
When I see past me to him as he is now

After some months, I found that I was compartmentalizing my feelings of loss so that I could cope with real life and get reengaged. But I discovered that it didn't work very well. The process of letting go of Luke was permeated with guilt. How could I relinquish his memory to the grave—or to the urn of his ashes that I placed in the cabinet because I couldn't bear to look at it without feeling undone?

My personal experiences with nonphysical consciousness have shown me that life is not confined to the body. Yet, the connection is gone, and my son is dead.

In a calmer state of mind, I recognized the narcissism—my indulgence in a very shallow view of life. I realized that I needed to explore the deeper pool of existence beyond my simple reflection. But that would have to wait. And I couldn't scatter his ashes in the ocean off the beach where we used to play; I couldn't let them go. They were all I had, even if I had to hide them from view. The pain and feelings of abandonment and confusion were still too strong.

Five O'clock Sadness

As I glimpse his image in a photo on the shelf
The sadness rebounds
It reverberates and echoes
In the hollow place of my soul

My heart is still lost
In the bottomless void
That once was the place
Where he and I communed

This place inside
Where he lived each day
Where I experienced his essence
And understood his soul

I'm weary of the sadness
Wondering when it will end
A mere thought drains me of life
It is a loss that has no recompense

I titled this lyric "Five O'clock Sadness" because that was the time when I wrote it—due to an experience that caught me off guard. I had glimpsed at a photo of Luke on a shelf, and the time on a nearby clock was the time of day when he died. The original opening to this piece was, "it has been ninety-eight days at about this hour that my son, my love, my friend departed."

I asked myself, "Why do I still feel this pain? Will I ever move forward to a new place? Or am I just stuck here?"

I used to sail, and every sailor knows the experience of being "in irons." That is when the wind calms to the point where there isn't enough power to move forward. It is a feeling of being stalled, adrift. And, unless you have oars, there is nothing you can do but wait for the wind to return. And that is how it felt. This was a place of weariness, fatigue, exhaustion, lethargy, and disillusionment—and I had no oars.

Over time, as I gave myself permission to be here without judgment, I found that the winds slowly, almost imperceptibly, picked up; and distracted by the daily routines of life, I discovered that I was moving forward on a subtle breath of air. I learned a lot about being present with myself without judgment—how important it is to the healing process, how it is the key to moving forward to a new place.

Hanging Pictures

Evoking emotions
Too difficult to grasp
Evoking thoughts
Too painful to bear

Reminiscence, nostalgia
What was, what isn't
What won't be again

Hanging out by the wall
Hanging onto memories
Grasping a wisp of his presence
I'm too hung up to hang up his pics

It's still too painful
It's still too sad
It's still too much to endure

A number of months following the "Five O'clock Sadness," Margot asked whether I was comfortable hanging Luke's photographs back on the walls. I found myself resisting the thought, since I'm the one who asked that they be removed. I felt that I should be past the grieving and celebrate his life, but I wasn't there yet.

A picture is worth a thousand words, or a million emotions. Even after all this time, my emotions were still raw. I felt guilty. I should have been past it. But I wasn't. I didn't languish in nostalgia and I was very aware that life was different now. I found I could be happy most of the time, but I still wasn't ready to walk down a hall or into a room, only to be reminded of the love I lost.

Eviscerated

It's hard, it's deep
The keen blade
That severed Luke from our lives
Eviscerated our family too

The head is here
The arms are there
The legs akimbo in a tree
And our innards are poured onto the ground

Our nerves are exposed
We recoil at touch
The pain of our loss
Magnified by each other's presence

We care so much
That we dare not speak
Lest we plunge that keen blade
Deeper into our wounds

We communicate with silence
Our teary eyes, our stooped shoulders
A sad smile, a quiet nod
It is our consolation to one another

We are looking for our heart
It seems to be lost
But, we know it is there
Somewhere in this darkness

It still beats, we hear it
It is a soft, quiet sound
Beckoning us back to a place
That is whole and warm and happy

It's hard, It's deep
I hope, I hope we find it

It was so hard to discuss the loss with my family. Not only because of the pain it evoked, but because I didn't want to focus on the loss. No matter how prepared, how aware, how knowledgeable we were about death and loss, the experience was harsh on our family. Words of consolation were too painful to speak, even a knowing look seemed cruel. We didn't avoid talking about Luke, but, for me, it had to be in very small doses. The memories were just too powerful, the loss so keenly felt. It was as if our hearts had retreated, our connections felt forced, and the warmth we had known had grown cold. But we knew we loved each other. So, moment-to-moment, we were patient, forgiving, loving, quiet, and listening.

After I wrote "Eviscerated," it offered a new level of conversation between us as we sought to achieve balance between remembering, recognizing, letting go, and moving forward.

Casualties of Loss

When the fabric of emotional devotion
Becomes worn and threadbare
Through tragedies and the cruel turns of life
Can it still hold true amid the turmoil of loss?

Loss that reverberates through memories of what once was
Loss of identity and purpose and place
Loss evident in the tattered and torn fabric of life
That overwhelms the soul during moments of reflection

I awake from a fugue to a damp, dull morning
As the fog clears to reveal a strange landscape
My sense of self evaporates with its mist
I am lost without and within, my true north is gone

I await the sun to warm my bones
To illuminate the path toward a new paradise
I look to my intimate, my travel companion, wounded and sad
I touch her gently or not at all, for it only evokes pain

Will she take another path than I?
Will our discoveries lead us apart?
Will our threadbare emotions find a healing balm?
Or will we remain forever lost to one another?

Our family was a casualty of Luke's death. The connections that seemed to come so naturally before were broken. As we tried to make sense of our lives without Luke, as we adjusted to a new life, I felt like I had also lost my family—especially the deep connection that I had shared with Margot. This was the beginning of another unanticipated journey—one in which the outcome was far from sure.

Fishing for Happiness

Happiness, like an oily fish
Pulled from the sea of hope
Slips through my grasp
Falling back into a churning oblivion

Shit!

It took a while for me to realize that I hadn't resolved as much as I had hoped, and found I had slid backwards. I had talked about happiness and its importance, but it took a lot of time to integrate it into my life. Now that I resolved to be happy again, I became conscious of all the new realities that would challenge it—especially how our family unit had been disrupted, how we had become disconnected as we each went through our own grieving processes and tried to adjust to a family without Luke.

In this vulnerable (and cranky) state, I was mad at happiness. I was fishing for it in a sea of hope, and no matter how hard I tried, it was oily and slippery and I couldn't hang on to it. So it falls back into the sea, which was no longer a sea of hope, but a churning oblivion, colored with hopelessness.

Walks

We take walks now
Margot and I
The undertone of loss lingering
In our voices, our sighs

The quiet walks
Evoke a newness of life
While recalling the loss of one
In the silence between our words

Words, sweet kind words,
Searching for a new perspective
A renewed relationship
Longing to feel whole again

How can we be complete?
When our family is not?
Still. We continue to walk
To talk, to be silent, to hope

Getting used to walks without Luke was very difficult. Luke had a jog stroller and we would often walk and roller blade around the neighborhood with him. Margot and I walking alone together was odd, and painful. Our walks became a small ritual of getting used to being together without him.

Margot

Deeply caring
Strong hearted
Open to wounds
Tough as nails

Beauty plumbs her depths
Touches others' hearts
Resonates with their longings
Heals their souls

Flickering glimpses of a love we know
Hidden beneath obligations and distractions
Layers upon layers of complex emotions
Approaching, then holding, awaiting, in love

Margot and I had been together nearly thirty years when we lost Luke. Our relationship was rooted in deeply caring for one another and appreciation for each other as individuals. Our relationship was deep and rich.

Over the course of Luke's life, as Margot gave up her life and career for Luke, being his champion and advocate; as I spent time with Luke on weekends to give Margot respite; and as our family life was Luke-centric, we may have lost some of our intimate connection. The emotional trauma of losing Luke took its toll. As we both grieved in our own ways, we discovered that the strain and distress had created a disconnection between us. With the centerpiece of our lives gone, we found we needed to rediscover our intimacy.

And though Luke was gone, our dear Lili remains a joyful, wonderful heartbeat in our home. Though her story is largely untold here, she brings us great joy each day!

Breaking the Ice

Breaking the ice
To the difficult conversation
Risking a fall
Into a deep, cold abandon

Our affection is frozen
Within the cold ice
That encapsulated our hearts
When we lost our son

We care so deeply
Yet the strings of our hearts
No longer respond
To each other's gentle touch

Can we awaken?
Our intimacy and love?
When parts of our hearts
Are now missing?

Taking the plunge is our only option
Using kind words that cut like a knife
To excise the scars
That are choking our hearts

A careful incision
An icy-hot blade
A cry of anguish
And our hearts beat again

The blood is warm
The thirst returns
Little sips at first
To savor, to nurture

In the midst of listening one night, I suddenly realized for the first time with great clarity how sad I was that the affection Margot and I had shared was missing. It seemed so odd to me that I had not recognized it—only this deep sadness that I carried with me.

In that moment, I sat down with Margot and explained how I felt. It felt so risky to have this conversation—I not only felt vulnerable, but I was concerned that I might be misunderstood, or that Margot might feel blamed. Yet, I felt so strongly that I had hit upon something extraordinarily important that I had to take the chance. Even as I said the words, I felt their authenticity—no blame, no fault, just recognition of another loss, a casualty of the loss of Luke, a casualty that I wanted to rescue and restore.

As we talked, we also recognized that we shouldn't talk too much. Rather, we needed to let the power of the recognition settle in and find its own depth within us. After the conversation, I lay awake for some time as Margot proceeded to organize our storage area for most of the rest of the night.

But the next day, there was new life in our relationship—even without much sleep.

Resolving

There is light
He is here
I am at peace

Sometimes weird things just happen. Not that weird is bad. Sometimes weird is healing.

I try to meditate in the mornings. Several months after his passing, I had this experience of Luke's presence that helped me be at peace. Was it real? Was it my creation out of a need for resolution? I don't know. But I liked the peaceful part of it, so I went with it. It didn't matter to me whether it was in my head. It was in my "knowing" and that was enough for me to feel lighter.

Transition

The world is different now
The better parts of me that he evoked
Lay quiet and unattended
How do I wake them from their sleep?

It is in each day, each moment
That I seek them out
To learn to live in that love
On my own

Months seemed like an eternity, but I began to find my footing.

When I speak of my son, I say he made his transition. Yet, I am also in transition, moving to a new, unfamiliar place. With some of the intense pain abating, I began to recover the stability of my rational mind, and the ability to look at what Luke nurtured in me, to pay attention, to evoke it on my own, without his help.

Toward Wholeness

The vestiges of my grief pulsate quietly
Lapping on the shores of my consciousness
In gentle waves
Allowing me to breathe life again

My anguish is like a quieted ocean,
Deep, unplumbed, still
Until a memory escapes
Innocently from the depths like a bubble

Breaking the surface
It triggers a torrent
Creating tidal waves and rip currents
Emotions overwhelm me

I was surprised to recognize that a number of months had passed before I wrote another piece. The time seemed to have sped by as, in retrospect, I had made a shift out of melancholy. But, as this reveals, I was still vulnerable.

Just when I thought I was on course to a "normal" life, a simple recollection awakened feelings of grief and loss that were so painful they arrested me, detached me, and plunged me into a swirling whirlpool of memories that were lucid and real, as if Luke had died yesterday.

But those are less frequent now. There are longer moments of joy with my family that define most days. We can have fun and play without feeling sad. It just takes time.

Happiness

Daddy
Be Happy
Be Happy
Be Happy

I truly believe these words were from Luke. In a session with my dear friend, clairaudient emotional healer and Luke's godfather, Richard Damien, this message came through from Luke.

My first response upon hearing this was complex—with competing voices sounding off in my head. Yes, I long to hear from my son again. But, I really just want to feel him in my arms, resting his head upon my chest. The skeptical side of me wondered whether I am just pulling from the vapors this message because I want closure. And yet another side of me blurted out, "Be happy?" and then thinking, "Is that all you have to say after all of these months of emotional turmoil?" It feels simplistic. I want more. I want to feel some connection to you.

Yet, as I reflected on the simplicity of the words, as I said them softly to myself, I felt an emotional buzz—an opening. And in repeating them I recognized that it's just like Luke. He always was a guy of few words and was impatient when conversations turned into nattering. I resolved that he was just telling me in the simplest and most straightforward terms how to deal with all of this. Time to turn the corner, dad... be happy!

In Luke's words was a reminder (again) that circumstances are just circumstances. They don't control my experience. Yes, these circumstances powerfully impact me, but I can choose, and do choose, to cultivate happiness. As I repeat Luke's words as an invitation, I find happiness vibrates inside and I can radiate it out into the world. I'm not great at sustaining it, as the next disappointment may **evoke sadness and loss**. But I can return to it again and again, to find happiness and practice it.

Thanks, Luke. I've got this.

Boundless Love

A tranquil stillness
Alighted upon my heart
Gently awaking
A new consciousness

Softly, tenderly
Whispering sweetly
There is no loss
Love permeates all

Quietly, soothingly
The veil of silence billows
Allowing a glimpse
Of another realm

He is there
I am here
Connected forever
By boundless love

On this afternoon, like many others with nothing special going on, I suddenly—though with no feeling of surprise—became aware of a palpable connection to Luke.

Though I am fully conscious and firmly planted on the family room sofa, there is another level of awareness that has popped open. And I can see it with my mind's eye. It is like Luke was right there, across the room, just beyond the billowing veil, and we are connected. There is no sorrow or grief. Just a presence, a connection—with the impression that it is always there for us. It appears to me as I relax and allow. It is not fragile; it is comfortable and sound. And I smiled to myself as I recognized the secret to finding this place was to be happy.

It has now been nearly a year. Time's cruel balm has had its effect. I am not sad as I was for many months. I realize—as I have always known—that Luke and I have separate lives. I still feel deeply the effects of our parting of ways. He now resides beyond the billowing veil and I am here. Thoughts of Luke still evoke sadness, yet I appreciate and accept the realities and transience of life.

I can go on along my path. I can be fully engaged in my life. Margot, Lili, Jessica, and I have found new ways to be a family without Luke. Though it will take time for us to feel emotionally whole.

I have arrived at a place where I can say that it's okay. I have found my way through the dark sadness by writing about it, giving my tumultuous feelings a voice. In doing so, I have released them to the light of day, released them so that they don't linger unheard in my soul to weigh me down or entangle me.

Rebirth

The hole in my heart let in a gentle light
That warmed my soul and caressed my spirit

This soft light of love with moist tears of grief
Gave birth to a seed that lay dormant inside

As it bloomed to life in a tender, soft essence
This tired, weary shell surrendered its loss

Awake at last, born out of anguish
A lighter spirit arose to greet the light

Lighten Up

I'm lighter now
Somehow freed
From the languishing anguish that fettered by mind

It happened unsurprisingly
Yet oddly surprising
A simple release, unanticipated, not strange

The freedom from thoughts
Imposed from within
Attachments to fragments of nostalgia of then

A fresh, new world
A rebirth of sorts
I've followed Luke and now made my transition

At times I had wished that I would just wake up one morning and feel better. That I wouldn't feel the loss and sadness when I see a picture, or hear his name, or remember wonderful times.

Yet, it didn't happen that way for me. Instead, I've been surprised by something entirely unexpected. There is a new part of me that is blooming to life, still vulnerable, but full of new expectation, ready to venture out and embrace the future. It is a lighter and happier me that has been birthed while I have grieved. And there is a part of me that I am letting go, a part that clings to me but is passing away. As I nurture this "tender, soft essence" I find that I can begin to shed the "tired, weary shell" and let it surrender its loss.

I am not forgetting Luke. He is very alive in my heart and mind. Though the feelings of vulnerability remain, the memories of him are a bit more accessible with less sadness.

Pictures Everywhere

His smile, his eyes
Greet me from room to room
As his fun-filled laughter
Echoes in my mind

I take a moment to soak him in
To relish the memories that spring to mind
Though vulnerable as tears warm my eyes
I am no longer lost in grief

I am whole, almost complete
As I recognize that Luke is part of me
I am who I am because of him
I celebrate his life each day

It has been a long journey. The most important lesson I can share is to allow yourself to grieve in your own way. We are all different, and if we try to impose rules upon ourselves, we may never discover a true resolution.

Our family has healed—though I still have work to do. To listen better, to be more present, to demonstrate in my words and actions how I feel in my heart. It is an investment that pays great dividends.

I am happy to see Luke's pictures on the wall. They now bring me joy and happiness—though not without tears. A big part of my healing was to recognize that my life with Luke changed me. I became a better person because of him and so I feel him within me as I reflect on that. I never understood it when people said "he will live in your heart" until now. Luke is alive within me—heart, mind, and soul—his energy, his laughter, his warmth, and the lessons I learned from him. I am a very lucky man.

The Luke Andrew Mueller Pediatric Palliative Care Fund
at
Joe DiMaggio Children's Hospital

There are few experiences in life more stressful than when your child is ill. The Luke Andrew Mueller Pediatric Palliative Care Fund in the Joe DiMaggio Children's Hospital Foundation provides support to hospitalized children and their families dealing with chronic and life-threatening conditions and illnesses.

If you are interested in contributing to the fund, contact:

Joe DiMaggio Children's Hospital Foundation
3329 Johnson Street
Hollywood, FL 33021 USA
Phone: 954-265-3454

Or, donate online:

https://www.jdch.com/about/foundation/give/donate

(When completing the donation form, please select "Other" in the Designation section, then type "Luke A. Mueller Fund")

I participated in Art4Healing workshops at JDCH where my infant son lay critically ill for months in the Pediatric ICU. The workshops supported my emotional well-being as I dealt with grief, fear, and stress. They also gave me a greatly needed break from my bedside vigil and a chance to interact with other parents who have told me that they, as well as their hospitalized children, also enjoyed and benefitted from the program. Thank you to the donors who made this possible.

—Amy (Parent)

I am a music therapist at JDCH. Today I helped a mom and the two sisters of a five-month-old terminally ill girl create a "Heartbeat Song." A few weeks earlier, when Dr. Meister and I mentioned the heartbeat song concept to the mom, she began to cry and made it her mission to get her two girls here (seven and ten years old) to create the song. So, using a recording of the child's heartbeat, the family created their own song to preserve her memory and legacy—a process now used by music therapists around the world. Mom is very active in memory making, using music therapy, photography, and other services available at Joe DiMaggio to create lasting memories of her daughter. This program is one of the most touching and meaningful projects I have been involved in. Thanks to the Luke Mueller Fund for making this possible.

—Stephanie, Music Therapist, JDCH

Lyrics of a Broken Heart: A Father's Journey Toward Wholeness
by James Mueller

Published by:
    James Mueller & Associates LLC
    Delray Beach, Florida USA

Copyright © 2020 by James Mueller

Book editing, design, and layout: Stephen C. Nill, CharityChannel LLC

All rights reserved. No part of this book shall be reproduced, stored in a retrieval system, or transmitted by any means, electronic, mechanical, photocopying, recording, or otherwise, without written permission from the publisher. No patent liability is assumed with respect to the use of the information contained herein. This publication contains the opinions and ideas of its author. It is intended to provide helpful and informative material on the subject matter covered. It is sold with the understanding that the author and publisher are not engaged in rendering professional services in the book. If the reader requires personal assistance or advice, a competent professional should be consulted. The author and publisher specifically disclaim any responsibility for any liability, loss, or risk, personal or otherwise, that is incurred as a consequence, directly or indirectly, of the use and application of any of the contents of this book. Although every precaution has been taken in the preparation of this book, the publisher and author assume no responsibility for errors or omissions. No liability is assumed for damages resulting from the use of information contained herein.

ISBN Hardcover Color Print Book: 978-1-7342973-0-0

ISBN Paperback Color Print Book: 978-1-7342973-2-4

13 12 11 10 9 8 7 6 5 4 3 2

www.ingramcontent.com/pod-product-compliance
Lightning Source LLC
Chambersburg PA
CBHW041220070526
44584CB00001B/23